Radford's House Designs of the Twenties

Wm. A. Radford Co.

Dover Publications, Inc.
Mineola, New York

How to Select a Home from This Book

A HUNDRED years ago there were plenty of building sites then for you to choose from and you could have chosen your home first and a place to put it on afterward. That is not so now. Where your house is to be built is almost as important as building it. The particular size lot, with the particular frontage or natural advantages which you want may not be available to you for several reasons. The kind of neighborhood, the distance from transportation, the conditions as regards paving, sewer, gas and electricity, etc., are some of the things that will govern your selection of a home-site. So we say pick out the place you want to build before you attempt to choose a house plan.

Fit the House to the Site

Having done that and with the lot in mind, try to find a house that will fit it. If it is a narrow lot, then you must have a narrow house; if it is a shallow lot, then you must find a plan that is not too deep from front to back but what it will not merely go on your lot but will leave a little room for a back yard and perhaps for a flower or vegetable garden, too.

Next, think about the orientation, or the direction the house will face. Try to have the principal rooms enjoy the most sunshine and air the year round. Secure for them the best views possible. See that the porch is where it will be the most usable at all times. Such matters as these are important and too often they are thought about after it is too late. Before you build is the time to correct such mistakes.

What Size House?

Now as to the size of the house. If you are like most people, you will begin with a big one and end with one much smaller. The cost will be a determining factor, no doubt, though not necessarily the final one. It is, instead, much more important that you fit your house to the requirements of your family than that your family be made to fit the house. Let the number of bedrooms decide. A house that won't sleep your family properly will, of course, not do. Whatever else you can have in the way of sun parlors, porches, toilets, "dens," etc., can be easily secured.

In this book there are nearly one hundred plans for moderate sized homes of the kind that most homebuilders like. There is enough variety in their exterior styles to suit every taste, and enough different room layouts for you to find not only one but possibly several houses that will exactly fit your lot, the requirements of your family, and your pocketbook.

The Plus Value of These Plans

But that isn't all that these plans offer you. Mere matters of size and layout, important as they are, have not been enough for the designers of these homes. They have sought to give you more, in the form of those little niceties of home planning which particular people appreciate, such as closets, downstairs lavatories, fireplaces, balconies, downstairs bedrooms for servants, easy and convenient communication between rooms, step-saving arrangements in the kitchen, and a hundred other little things that mean more livability in your home. These are the things that don't cost much extra, sometimes nothing extra, yet they mean much in comfort and convenience. Years of experience are necessary to know how to get these big little extras into a plan and still hold down the cost.

It is just such experience which has gone into the planning of these homes. Naturally, to make sure that you get the full benefit of that knowledge, you will want to have complete plans for building your house. Only in that way can you avoid mistakes and at the same time assure yourself that the house when finished will look just as it does in the book.

See Your Lumber Dealer About Costs

It is only by using a complete plan, too, that you can get a definite estimate on the cost of building your home. All other figures are but guesses and it is dangerous to guess when building, no matter how experienced in building the guesser is.

The proper person to give you a definite, reliable estimate on your home is your local lumber dealer or builder. Consult him; get the benefit of his advice on homebuilding conditions as they obtain in your community. He will tell you and his counsel will be as reliable as any can be, for your permanent satisfaction is his concern and he will see that you get it.

Finally, remember that in homebuilding as in everything else, you cannot have everything you want. Compromises have to be made somewhere and probably more have to be made when building a home than in anything else. So don't give up too easily. You will find some house in this book which will come as near fitting your specifications as probably any house possibly could and in time you will probably find it fitting them better than you imagined.

Build it! Begin now to know the pleasure of living in a house suited to your own requirements, and to know the satisfaction of owning your Home!

Bibliographical Note

This Dover edition, first published in 2003, is an unabridged republication of the work originally published by Radford, Chicago, in 1925 under the title *Home Builders' Red Book*.

International Standard Book Number: 0-486-42993-8

Manufactured in the United States of America
Dover Publications, Inc., 31 East 2nd Street, Mineola, N.Y. 11501

AN INDIVIDUAL DUTCH COLONIAL

THIS house is of excellent design, and it has individuality in the treatment of the dormers. Inside, the plan is entirely up to the promise of the exterior, particularly in the service portion, where you will find a back stairway, a downstairs toilet, and a large kitchen pantry. Other features are the den and the three fireplaces. With the porch toward the street this house can go on a 40-foot lot and it will look well from any angle.

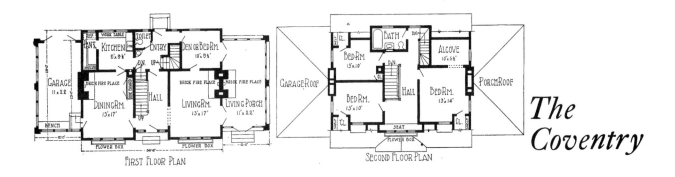

The
Coventry

3

FOR EITHER A WIDE OR A NARROW LOT

N O matter what kind of a site you have for your house, this little bungalow is pretty apt to fit it. If the lot is as narrow as 30 feet, put the dining room-porch end toward the street; if you have a wide but shallow lot, put the broadside toward the street. And you can face this house in any direction.

The
Waldo

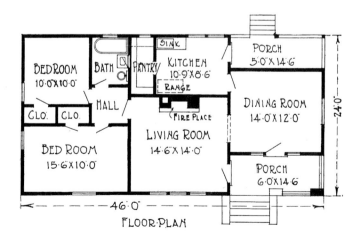

FLOOR·PLAN

DO YOU BELIEVE THE DINING ROOM IMPORTANT?

THE one in this house is unusually situated, of large size and of convenient proportions. It is distinct from the living room and, because a pantry and hall intervenes between them, from the kitchen. It has its own outlet to the front hall and a broad triple window that makes it bright and easily ventilated at all times. Of course there are other important points about this plan, too, but the dining room is worth special attention.

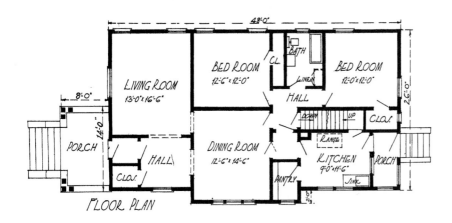

FLOOR PLAN

The Shawnee

5

ONLY SKILLFUL PLANNING COULD PRODUCE SUCH A SECOND FLOOR LAYOUT

AS you can see from the plan, the main body of this house is only 28 by 27 feet on the ground. The second floor ceiling line is really less, because this is a story-and-a-half house. Yet, you have here three bedrooms, the two smaller having considerably over one hundred square feet each of floor space. In addition, you have five closets extraordinarily large, even with cut ceilings. After all, it's the number and size of the bedrooms that is the index to the size of a house, and here is one that scores high. The Morley will fit a 35 or 40-foot lot.

The Morley

FIRST FLOOR PLAN   SECOND FLOOR PLAN

HOSPITABLE COLONIAL BUNGALOW

DON'T you think there is something especially inviting about this handsome home? It is hard to analyze it, but considering that this is merely a simple design, with no extraordinary amount of frills and frolls, we must conclude that we like this because it is just what it pretends to be—a fair-sized, hospitable-looking house, built for comfort-loving folks. There is ample closet space everywhere, and the kitchen is so well shelved as to eliminate the need for a pantry. Wide Colonial siding, painted white, is proper for this exterior, and the trellises for vines set off the terraced French doors nicely.

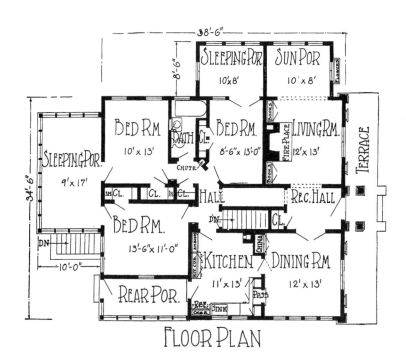

FLOOR PLAN

*The
Farwell*

TWO "MASTER" BEDROOMS ARE OFFERED YOU IN THIS PLAN

ONE of them has a dressing room in connection, a supplementary room which the housewife will appreciate, for it will help to keep the bedroom tidy and free from the signs of living, and by providing a place for certain pieces of furniture will enable you to make something of an upstairs living room of the front chamber. Notice that all the bedrooms have cross-corner light and ventilation and each is close to the bathroom and the stairway. An attic stair reached through the closet of the front bedroom makes the third floor available for storage purposes. The first floor of The Bagley has its conveniences, too. The reception hall makes the front door directly accessible from the kitchen and provides easy communication with the stairway. The kitchen is well thought out, with its daylight pantry and vestibule.

The Bagley

FIRST & SECOND FLOOR PLANS

EIGHT ROOMS PLUS A SUN PARLOR AND SLEEPING PORCH

AND they are good big porches, too, the sleeping porch being large enough for two beds, and it is directly connected with two bedrooms. Something unusual for a sleeping porch is the closet. Another unusual feature of this house is the fact that the bedrooms are all of the same size; no one has sacrificed space for the sake of any other; all are livable, of good proportions, and lighted and ventilated from windows on two sides. Study the downstairs, too. There's a toilet at the end of the hall. The maid can reach the front door or the stairway from the kitchen without going through the dining room. A vestibule provides protection from the weather to you or your guests before being admitted. The living room and library are both directly connected with the sun parlor and are separated by a wide opening that makes one room in effect of the two. In addition to these conveniences, there's a storage attic reached by a full-sized stairway.

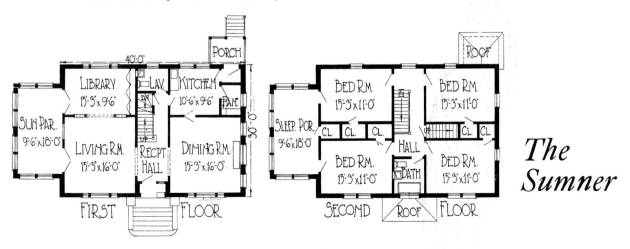

The Sumner

UNIQUE TREATMENT OF THE FRONT ENTRANCE AND STAIR

YOU don't come directly into the living room from the big front porch of this house, nor is there a hall. There is a sort of inside-outside vestibule that protects both the privacy and comfort of the living room. The closed stairway is secluded and in turn gives privacy to the downstairs bedroom. The wide cased opening between the dining room and living room makes practically one big room out of them.

The Stilwell

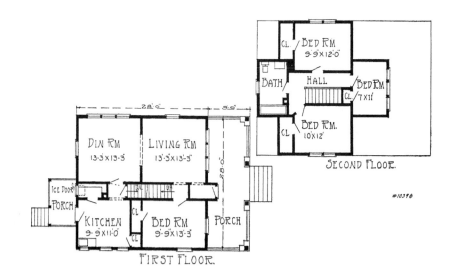

COTTAGE COMFORT AND BEAUTY

COTTAGE comfort and beauty are shown in this plan and design, attractive through the wide sweep of the roof and the covered entry. And this is a plan which might have the first floor finished as the initial building operation with the bedrooms on the second floor left unfinished until more room was needed, since the first floor alone will serve the needs of the family. The sun porch adds much to the size of the living room with its pleasant fireplace, the dining room is of an adequate size, and the bedrooms well grouped with the bath. The two bedrooms on the second floor are well proportioned and adequately provided with closet space.

The Lambert

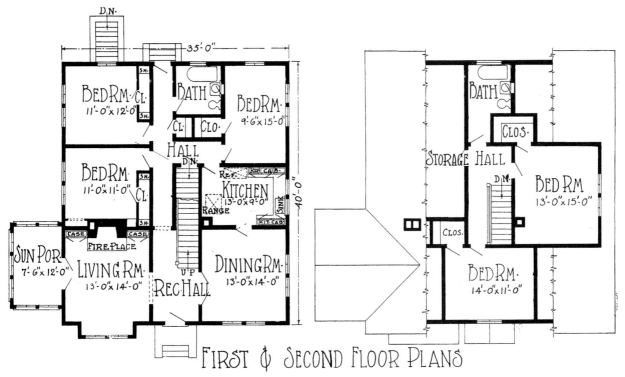

FIRST & SECOND FLOOR PLANS

PRIVACY FOR BOTH SLEEPING AND LIVING QUARTERS IN THIS BUNGALOW

YOU have seen some bungalows in which bedrooms opened directly onto the living room, or the bathroom was plainly in evidence, or the front door spoiled a good portion of the living room. These defects are not to be found in The Hensley. A vestibule provides protection for the living room, keeping cold blasts of air from hitting the room directly. It has a closet for coats—an essential to the one-floor plan. Placing the basement stairway where it is here is the secret of the success of this plan. It divides the house in two and separates the parts by two walls and some three or four feet of space. This division carried on through to the kitchen produces a large closet for the back bedroom and a ventilated pantry for the kitchen. This kitchen, you will notice, has a window in each of two adjoining walls. Now look at the porch. The entrance to it and the house are at one and the same end. That leaves most of the porch space available as an outdoor living room for warm weather.

The Hensley

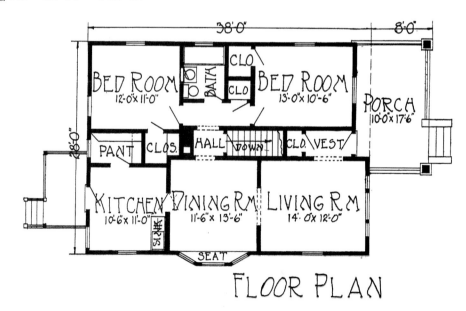

FLOOR PLAN

HOUSEKEEPING IS EASIER WITH SUCH A KITCHEN

THE room is of the right size and shape for efficient work. It is bright and easily ventilated because of the two windows over the sink. The built-in cupboard at the end of the sink can contain utensils, dishes and supplies constantly used. Other things can be put in the big pantry, with its generous cupboard and table space. The pantry has its own window and the icebox is placed for icing from the outside. The vestibule can be shut off from the kitchen but the outside door can be left open for the ice man and for the grocer boy, who can put his packages on a table beneath the vestibule window. Brooms, sweepers and cleaners can go in the open closet at the head of the basement steps.

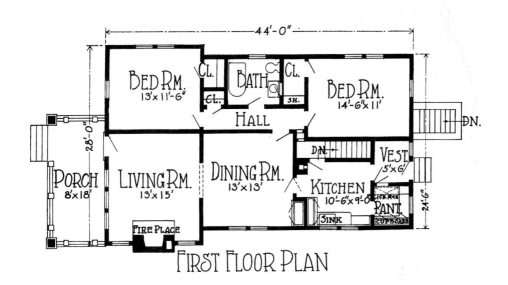

FIRST FLOOR PLAN

The
Elmore

PROFESSIONAL MEN! HERE'S A SUGGESTION

NOTE the "den" shown on the plan. If you need an office in your home, it should make a good one. Cut a door through the reception hall and your patients or clients wouldn't have to enter your home at all. The large reception hall has a closet for coats and a chair or two might even be placed in it for the comfort of your callers. Atwood has a good layout in other respects, too, but the plan does not show this office possibility.

The Atwood

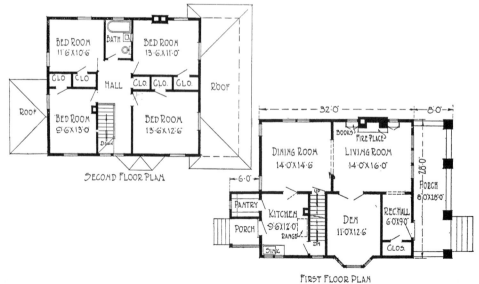

AN EFFICIENT SIX ROOM HOUSE

THE thrifty Dutch colonists early developed in America a type of home which allows for the utilization of all of the floor space in a manner that later builders have found hard to equal or excel in other types of architecture. The gambrel roof allows the full use of the floor space of the second story without awkward ceiling slopes and angles. The Dutch Colonial illustrated here is made especially attractive by the careful placing of the windows and the arched roof of the entryway, which gives a pleasing contrast to the predominating straight lines of the house. The interior arrangement is typical of the Colonial home, with an attractive living room and sun parlor on one side of the reception hall and the dining room and kitchen on the other. There are three large bedrooms on the second floor.

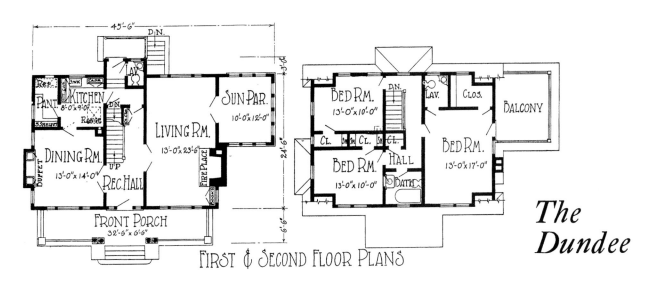

FIRST & SECOND FLOOR PLANS

The Dundee

A SPANISH MISSION DESIGN FOR A THIRTY-FOOT LOT

THERE is no pretense about this type of house. It is simplicity itself. Just four walls and a roof and an invisible flat roof at that, but one covering the absolute maximum of floor space with the minimum of roof area. The arches over the openings to the porch, the strip of roof tile over the front casements, and the downspouts are the only details of this building which might be considered ornamental. It depends solely on its good proportions and these details for its attractiveness. Don't you think the result successful? Inside, there is individuality, too. Both dining room and living room are connected with the porch but are not themselves thrown together. The breakfast nook is especially private and the kitchen odors and noises are not apt to penetrate to the dining and living rooms. With all these conveniences, The Gilboa can be built in most communities on a lot as narrow as thirty feet.

The Gilboa

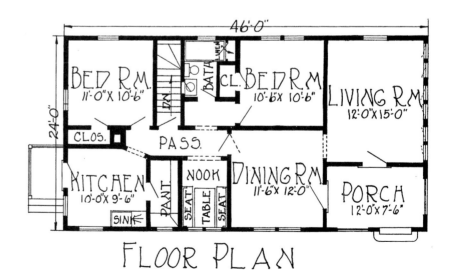

FLOOR PLAN

EVERY ROOM HAS WINDOWS ON TWO SIDES, EVEN THE KITCHEN

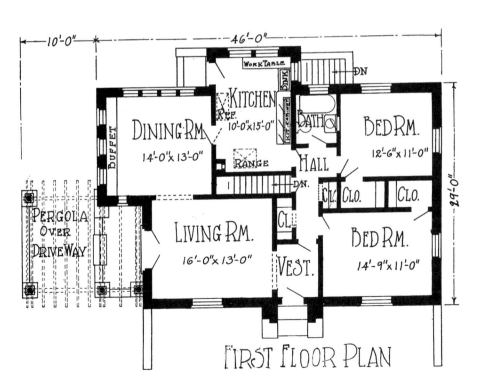

FIRST FLOOR PLAN

THE dining room has a small opening on a third side even. Such provision for light and air make this house adaptable to any latitude. The rooms will be bright in winter and cool in summer. The Natchez is a house that can face the north if need be, for there is no porch to shut off light from the living room. The arrangement of the bedrooms and bath is most convenient and gives them complete separation from the rest of the house. There is a closet for the vestibule and another for linen. The pergola can be omitted if the lot requires it.

The Natchez

TWO BIG BEDROOMS UPSTAIRS FOR EMERGENCY USE

THE first floor of The Galena is a splendid plan in itself but it is supplemented so generously by the upper part of this story-and-a-half house that the facilities of the latter must not be overlooked. One of the second floor bedrooms has two closets on one side and a dressing alcove on the other, making it in these respects the most desirable chamber in the house. There is a toilet upstairs in addition to the full bath room downstairs. The location of the stairways and having them run parallel with the front rather than the side of the house makes a handy arrangement possible for the downstairs bedrooms and bath. These rooms have privacy from the living quarters, and yet are easily reached from the rest of the house. Possibly the most important point about this plan, however, is the fact that it will go on a lot even narrower than 35 feet.

FIRST FLOOR PLAN   SECOND FLOOR PLAN

The Galena

MAKING THE MOST OF THE STORY-AND-A-HALF HOUSE

IF the floor plans of The Ingalls were not shown you here, you would probably turn the page and look no further into this house, assuming it is too small to suit your requirements. It would be a mistake to pass it up, however, if you are looking for an inexpensive house with three or four bedrooms. Yes, The Ingalls has three or four bedrooms—four, if you wish to use the spare room downstairs as such—in spite of the fact that it covers a ground area of less than nine hundred square feet! If need be, you could put the end of the house to the street, entering the porch from the end rather than the side, and build The Ingalls on a 40-foot lot. In spite of its numerous rooms, every part of this house is skillfully arranged. The living room is large, with a fireplace at one end, and one of the spare room closets can be used for coats; a wide cased opening between the dining room and living room makes both seem larger; and there is a big pantry for a good-sized kitchen.

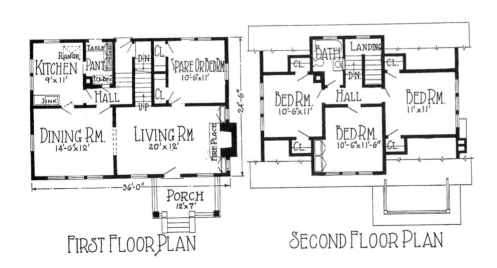

FIRST FLOOR PLAN   SECOND FLOOR PLAN

The Ingalls

A SATISFYING DESIGN IN BRICK

EVEN such a slight detail as the stucco and timbered construction of the gable ends of this substantial dwelling helps to set off the brick walls and add to the attractiveness of the whole. It is a type of home which naturally appeals to the substantial type of home-owner everywhere. Placing the entrance at the side gives full breadth of room to the handsome sun parlor—a 10-foot by 24-foot room extending across the front of the house. A French door opening helps to make it seemingly one with the living room, if such is desired. The whole floor plan in other respects is admirable; the spacious dining room; the breakfast room; the kitchen, with its own rear vestibule; the two amply dimensioned bedrooms which adjoin the bathroom across the small central hall.

The
Jackson

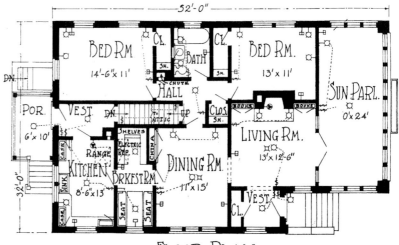

FLOOR PLAN

A VERY ATTRACTIVE SMALL HOUSE

A HOUSE of the sort that will appeal to folks wishing the maximum of housing effectiveness without the outlay of any excess expenditure for "frills." The roomy porch, recessed under the small extension gable, is roomy and inviting. It gives access direct into the living room, fitted with a fireplace and a window seat that has many decorative possibilities. A colonnade or French door arrangement separates from the dining room—well-lighted, with windows on two sides. The kitchen has the working parts, such as the sink, cabinet, etc., placed where they will get the full benefit of light from the two windows, and the refrigerator is so placed as to have its ice placed in through the icing door from the porch outside.

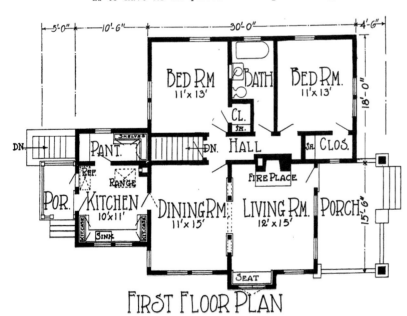

FIRST FLOOR PLAN

The
Oneida

DAYLIGHTED CLOSETS FOR BOTH OF THESE BEDROOMS

SUNLIGHT and air are good for clothes as well as bodies. Garments kept in closets with outside windows which are frequently opened are always fresh and sweet for use. Besides, the windows in these closets help to ventilate the rooms. Because of the location of the two stairways in The Kelton, the sleeping quarters have unusual privacy. Only one door separates them from the rest of the house. This door can be locked at night and the bedrooms shut off with comparative security. Another conspicuous feature of this plan is the unusually large pantry. Would you prefer to make the outside end of it into a dining nook, leaving a pass-pantry between the nook and kitchen? The space is large enough and it can be easily done. With the cases at the ends of the sink the kitchen itself has storage space for dishes and kitchen supplies. A big back porch is a part of this plan which will always be appreciated.

The Kelton

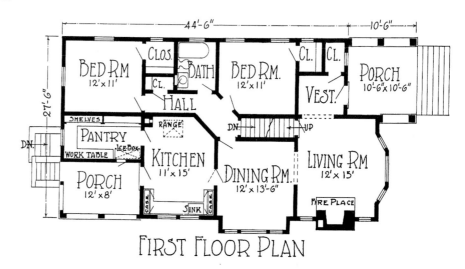

FIRST FLOOR PLAN

BORROWING AN IDEA FROM THE APARTMENT HOUSE

YOU think nothing of a flat roof on an apartment house, do you? Why should the advantages of such a roof be denied the individual home or single-family house? It is economical in construction, requiring a very minimum of materials, and if it is handled right a small single-family house with a flat roof can look attractive, too. The Oakland is a daring example of this sort of thing. It offers the maximum of house for the minimum cost of roof. Just see what you do get inside here; a very large dining room, with windows on three sides, and a fireplace; a dining room whose dimensions are appealing to the family that likes to entertain at meals; two commodious bedrooms, and a kitchen up-to-date in every particular, including a daylight pantry with a refrigerator for outside icing.

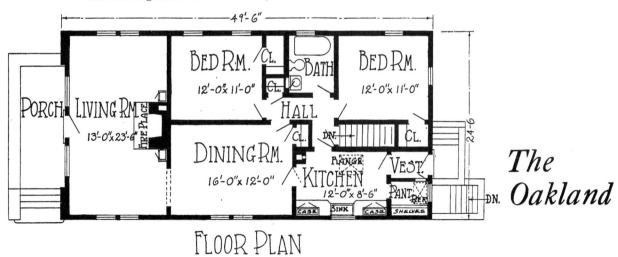

The Oakland

FLOOR PLAN

A LIBRARY DOWNSTAIRS AND TWO BATHROOMS UPSTAIRS

The Quincy

LIVING rooms that must serve as libraries too are not always satisfactory to the book-loving family. They want a place where those who want to can read in quiet and peace, and it is a rare family indeed whose members all feel like reading at the same time. In The Quincy the library is a separate room from the living room and being in the back of the house has a seclusion which it deserves. It has plenty of wall space for shelves, while at the same time it has windows on two sides to make it bright in the winter and cool in summer. The rest of the downstairs is equally well planned, too, while upstairs a special feature is the two bathrooms and the sleeping porch and fireplace for the master's bedroom.

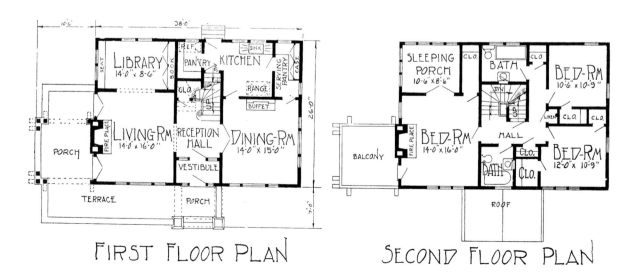

FIRST FLOOR PLAN   SECOND FLOOR PLAN

LOTS OF HOUSE FOR A 28-FOOT FRONTAGE

YOU will probably have difficulty in finding a place that offers you so much for so little as this one. The house can go on a 40-foot lot or less, and a very shallow lot at that, for it is not a long house, yet you have four bedrooms upstairs and on the first floor the regulation rooms plus a porch, a library and a pantry. These rooms, while not huge, are of pretty good size, plenty big enough for comfortable living. Such an advantageous arrangement is possible, of course, because of the shape of the house. It is nearly square, a fact which also means that it would be an economical house to build. In spite of the large number of bedrooms, careful planning has found space for good closets for all of them. Two of the chambers have two closets each, while a third has one big closet running back under the attic stair, and the occupant of the fourth bedroom can use the closet in the hall.

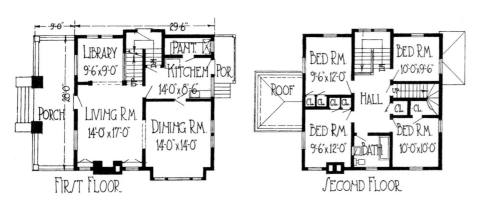

The Randall

WALL SPACE FOR LIVING ROOM FURNITURE

THE lack of it is no laughing matter, but a serious detraction from the livability of a room. Have you a piano? If so, how about the corner of the living room opposite the fireplace? If you have a davenport or a large library table, think how it would look along the wall opposite the entrance, where it would be the first thing seen on entering and thus mold your impression of the room as a whole?

The Axtell

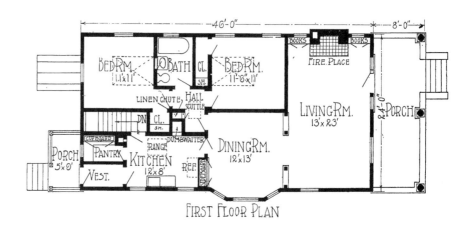

FIRST FLOOR PLAN

WHAT A BAY WINDOW DOES FOR A DINING ROOM

Y OU would hardly realize that the dining room in this house is an inside room, that is, not in a corner. This is because of the big bay window. It not only allows you to see to the front and back of the house, but it catches breezes and sunshine from two other directions that the room would not get without it. The additional floor space is also worth mention.

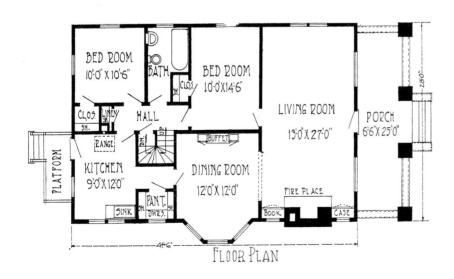

FLOOR PLAN

The Tuscola

GETTING AWAY FROM THE COMMONPLACE IN BOTH DESIGN AND PLAN

WHAT very striking effects can be produced from ordinary materials in the hands of some one who knows how, is illustrated in this attractive bungalow. Aside from its excellent proportions and the fact that the house hugs the ground it depends solely upon a modified form of half-timber work for ornament. The brick keystones around the entrance are also important for they not only furnish contrast with the lighter stucco, but also a color note of value to the exterior. The small panes in the windows and doors add interest to the openings and preserve the scale of the house. If you decide to build The Beaufort be careful about taking liberties with its design or plan, for you may unintentionally spoil some of its beauty. Keep it as close to the ground as it is here.

The Beaufort

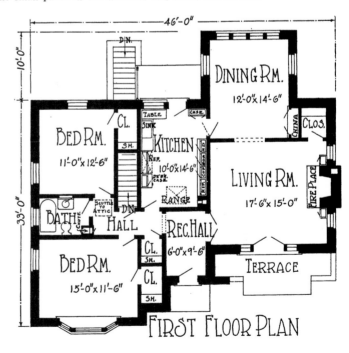

FIRST FLOOR PLAN

ANOTHER DESIGN AND PLAN WITH CHARACTER AND UNUSUAL QUALITIES

IT is the restraint shown in the design of this house which makes it attractive. Outside of the nice proportions of the house as a whole, the distinguishing details are the openings. They are tastefully treated and carefully spaced for the best effects. Of recent years a vogue for fancy roofs has arisen probably because composition shingles are so easily employed in a variety of effects. The rolled edges of this roof at both the eaves and gables are produced by such shingles, and the attractive result is due to the restraint with which the material is used, as previously suggested. From both the picture and plan of The Racine you will notice that the house, while especially adapted to a corner lot will also fit an inside lot and a comparatively narrow one at that.

FLOOR PLAN

The Racine

29

A CORNER LOT IS THE PROPER SETTING FOR THIS HOUSE

IT is plain from a study of this plan that the "L" shaped house has interesting possibilities, particularly for the corner lot. For one thing, the entrance in the angle between the two wings is equally accessible from all parts of the house, and at the same time cuts down hall space. The living room and dining room are far apart, a genteel arrangement when guests come for meals. Both rooms have windows on their sides which look out upon the streets and insure light and air inside. In The Amity space is found downstairs for a bedroom and bath for the maid. Upstairs are three bedrooms and a bath for the family. The large closets of these bedrooms add much to their enjoyment and the situations of the chambers at the ends of the halls give each a privacy that cannot be obtained in the bedrooms in the house of square or rectangular shape.

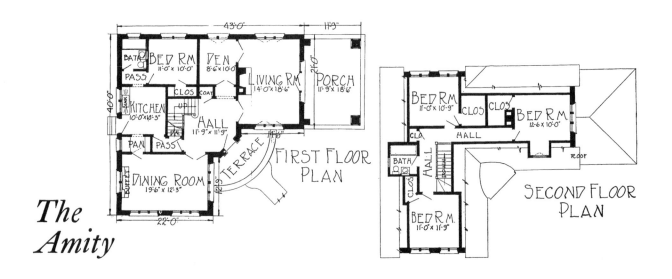

The Amity

A HOUSE WITH INDIVIDUALITY FOR A LARGE FAMILY

HERE is a house that merits careful study, both for the good taste shown in its exterior design and for the extraordinary skill evident in its planning. The closely cropped roof; the divided light windows, with a few diamond-paned sash; the little wrought-iron balcony for one of the bedrooms; and the monogram on the chimney are little details that add much to the beauty of the exterior. Look at the plan a moment. The vestibule, protected on three sides, removes the objection to the entrance opening upon the living room. The location of the stairway is unique and makes a secluded downstairs lavatory possible. The dining room is well placed with respect to all the downstairs rooms, including the servant's room. In addition to two full baths for the six bedrooms upstairs, one of the chambers has a toilet all its own.

The Chatham

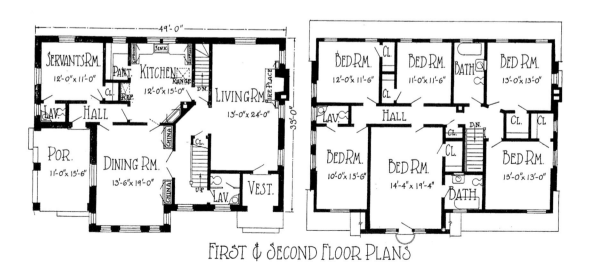

FIRST & SECOND FLOOR PLANS

A NARROW LOT HOUSE WITH WELL ARRANGED SERVICE QUARTERS

THE pergola shown in the picture makes The Ferndale look wider than it really is, for the house itself is only 24 feet wide and can therefore be built on a 30-foot lot. The house and pergola, too, can be built on a 40-foot lot. A noteworthy detail of this plan is the matter of the back entrance. One door is made to suffice for both grade and rear door. With this layout, there is easy communication between the basement and the outside, particularly appreciated on wash days or when carrying ashes out of the basement. Much mess is saved from the kitchen floor. Yet the stairway to the basement is not only under cover, but is completely enclosed and usable by anyone working in the kitchen. There is room enough at the top of the steps for the refrigerator where it can be iced without the iceman entering the kitchen.

The Ferndale

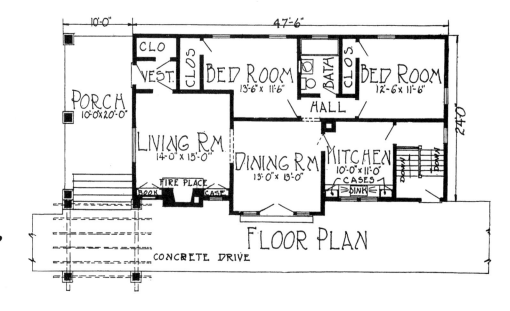

32

CHARMING DUTCH COLONIAL HOME

THIS type of house has about it a charm and hospitality that never fails to appeal. Built of frame with an attractive lattice effect on the lower story and drop siding above, it has distinctive roof dormers, arched in the center. The side entrance opens into a long reception hall. From this hall stairs lead direct to the upper floor while open doorways on either side give access to the large living room and dining room. The living room is 13 feet 3 inches by 27 feet extending the full depth of the house.

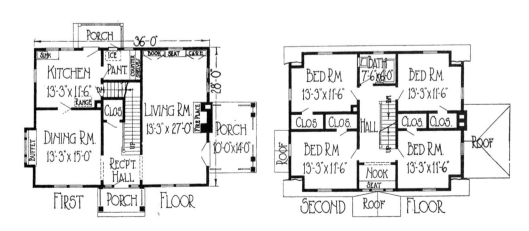

The Upton

THE ENGLISH COTTAGE STYLE OF BUNGALOW

NO question about it, this type of structure has come to stay, and it is not hard to account for its popularity. It is of a type which requires very little repair attention from year to year, and the look of it suggests substantial, comfortable living. The use of brick in combination with stucco timber construction gives a fine result, don't you think? The brick should be brown or maroon, preferably; the stucco, natural or cream colored; the timbered pattern, brown. This kind of house never calls for a large entrance porch, so a small vestibule leads into the entrance hall, with handsome stained wood staircase and coat closet. To the right is the living room, amply dimensioned, with fireplace. Off it is the dining room, with pergolaed terrace for summer dining.

The Danbury

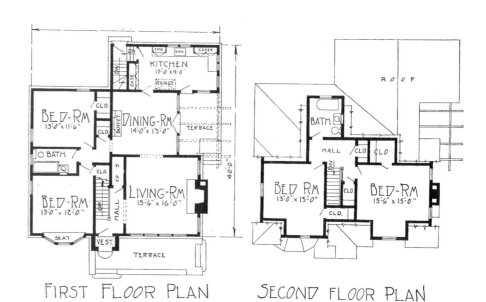

FIRST FLOOR PLAN   SECOND FLOOR PLAN

"SOMETHING DIFFERENT" FOR THE EXTERIOR WITHOUT EXTRA EXPENSE

YOU have no doubt noticed a marked tendency toward houses with less overhang at the eaves, and without useless ornamental details such as roof brackets, heavy porch posts and the like. Instead, houses of this and similar character are coming in—houses in which the principal claim to beauty lies in their good proportions and the restraint and good taste shown in their details. The Wooster is a design strongly suggestive of the French peasant cottage, but employing modern construction and materials. The front entrance is emphasized in an effective manner and the tiny balconies of the bedroom windows are other points of interest. The crenallated parapet above the sun parlor contrasts with the full, even sweep of the adjoining roofs. In spite of its spaciousness, The Wooster can be built on a 50-foot lot with room enough for driveway down the side. Hall space is saved inside and the entrance door placed almost at the foot of the open stairway which is of architectural importance to the living room. A bedroom and full bathroom connected are important features of the main floor. Three other bedrooms and another bath occupy the second floor and provide accommodations for a good sized family or for many guests.

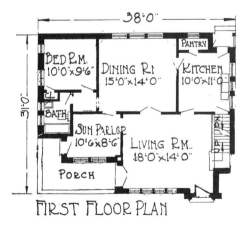

FIRST FLOOR PLAN

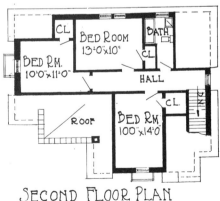

SECOND FLOOR PLAN

The Wooster

A SUBSTANTIAL, DIGNIFIED RESIDENCE

THIS house should appeal to the prospective homeowner who may have childhood associations that make the two-story dwelling still appeal as against the more modern bungalow. It is not too big, and does not make the work of housekeeping too great, but it presents a fine, dignified appearance, and an impression of well-proportioned interiors that the floor plans carry out. Downstairs, for instance, we have a nicely proportioned living room reached from a hall which has all the old-time decorative possibilities of an open staircase. The living room has a fireplace and light on three sides. Across the hall is the dining room, which connects directly with the kitchen. There is nothing old fashioned about this latter; it has every modern arrangement, using space to the utmost to give maximum convenience. Upstairs are three bedrooms and a bathroom, and a sewing room right at those three windows you see at the center of the second floor. Altogether, this is a substantial, dignified, extremely liveable home.

The Pulaski

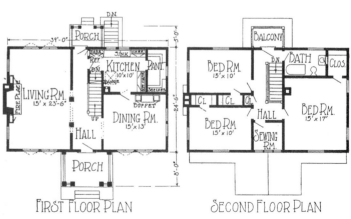

FIRST FLOOR PLAN   SECOND FLOOR PLAN

LOOK AT THIS MASTER'S BEDROOM!

IT is a "whale" in size and with windows on three sides abundantly lighted and ventilated and it is connected directly with the bathroom. But this bedroom is only a part of the house; the first floor is particularly well laid out. Due to the side entrance a porte cochere is possible for the outside and only a small reception hall is necessary inside. This makes a living room as large as the owner's bedroom. The Houston has a downstairs bedroom for the maid.

The Houston

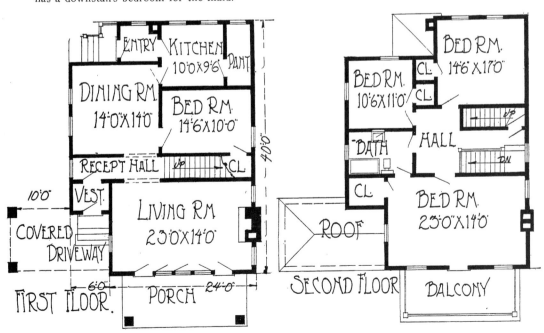

FIRST FLOOR.

SECOND FLOOR.

UNUSUALLY SPACIOUS BRICK RESIDENCE

THE bungalow lines of this dwelling deceive, for it contains many more rooms than other residences with seemingly more pretentious-spaced exteriors. There are eight rooms in all. Taking a look at the downstairs rooms we find that entrance is through a side vestibule that leads into a hall, and thence to the living room, 15 feet by 22 feet. There is fine lighting here from long French windows at either end, and also from the French doors that open onto the sun porch, so enclosed that it is virtually a ninth room. Through the hall again we are in the dining room, 11 feet by 14 feet, with a bay window, and connecting directly with the kitchen, 9 feet 6 inches by 11 feet. A doorway in the dining room leads to the two downstairs bedrooms, with their convenient toilet and lavatory. Upstairs we have three bedrooms, a storage room and a bathroom.

The Paxton

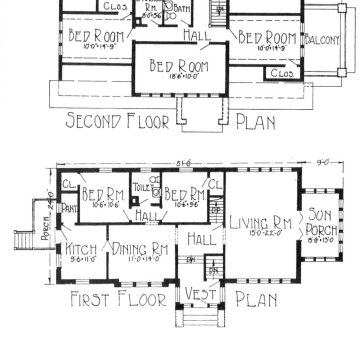

SEVEN ROOMS FOR A 35-FOOT LOT

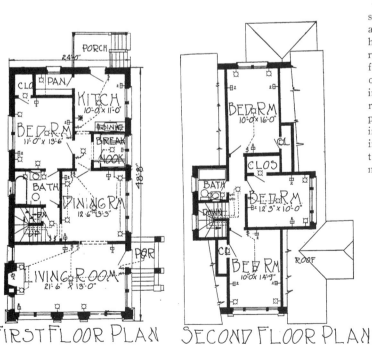

FIRST FLOOR PLAN   SECOND FLOOR PLAN

THREE spacious bedrooms and a bathroom are concealed in the upper part of this story-and-a-half house which looks more like a one-floor bungalow. The principal bedroom, however, is downstairs where it has a bathroom all its own. This bathroom is near the foot of the stairway so it can be used also by occupants of the second floor bedrooms. Having the entrance at one corner of the living room minimizes the disturbance of other occupants of the room caused by anyone coming in or going out. Because a breakfast nook intervenes between the dining room and kitchen there is little possibility of kitchen odors or noises reaching the living portion of the house.

The
Loomis

BOTH A DINING ROOM AND A DINING PORCH IN THE RADNOR

D INING alcoves or breakfast nooks have become quite common in recent years. They
will probably become a permanent part of our homes, too, because of their convenience
and the time and steps they save in serving informal meals. It is not often, however, that
you find a plan with a dining porch. Here is one. It has more than enough space for the
ordinary breakfast nook furniture, so it is likely you will enjoy a majority of your meals
here. On one side you look out on a terrace and on the other to the side yard or garden or
street. Besides this screened dining porch The Radnor also has a regular dining room, a room somewhat larger than in many houses of this size. A wide cased opening practically joins this room to the living room, making each seem larger than it is and enabling you to use them as one room when the occasion demands.

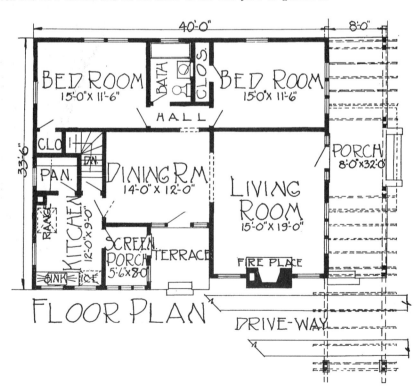

The
Radnor

OVER 230 SQUARE FEET OF LIVING ROOM

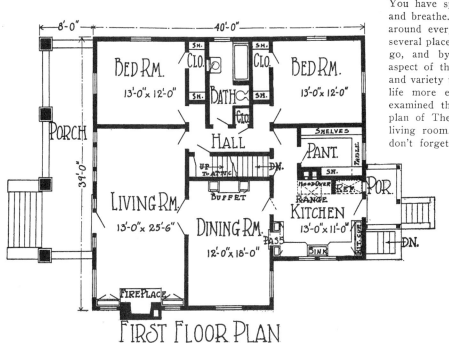

FIRST FLOOR PLAN

HAVE you ever had a living room 13 x 25½ feet in size? If not, you cannot realize the pleasure of living in such a room. You have space enough in which to move and breathe. You can change the furniture around every now and then, for there are several places where the different pieces will go, and by so doing change the whole aspect of the room. This all adds interest and variety to the daily existence and makes life more enjoyable. So, after you have examined the other good points about the plan of The Olivet, ponder a bit over the living room. But while you are doing it, don't forget that a 216-square foot dining room is right next to it, and further on still a kitchen and a pantry that provides plenty of work space and storage space for the hostess who is used to serving big meals and who is particular about the service quarters in her house.

The Olivet

MR. MAN! HOW ABOUT A ROOM FOR YOU WHERE NO WOMEN ARE ALLOWED?

DO you dare think of it? Would you have nerve enough first to suggest it and later to insist on it? If you have, then look at the "spare room" indicated on the plan. Like left-overs from a big meal, it is something free, being already paid for, and therefore no one will ever miss it or contest your right to it if

you claim it first. The only way anyone can get in or out of it is through a passageway from the living room which you can easily guard. There are no other openings except the windows, and so you will be completely shut off from disturbers and noises in the dining room and kitchen will even seem remote. Of course, if you can't prove your right to this room then it will probably go for an emergency bedroom, maid's room, library, sewing room or what not, supplementing the other spacious rooms of this compact house.

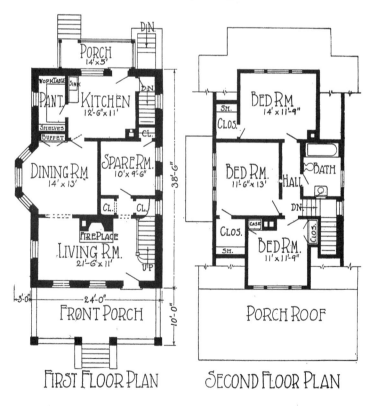

FIRST FLOOR PLAN   SECOND FLOOR PLAN

The
Murchison

42

COOL IN SUMMER AND LIGHT IN WINTER, FOR THE WINDOWS
GO CLEAR TO THE FLOOR

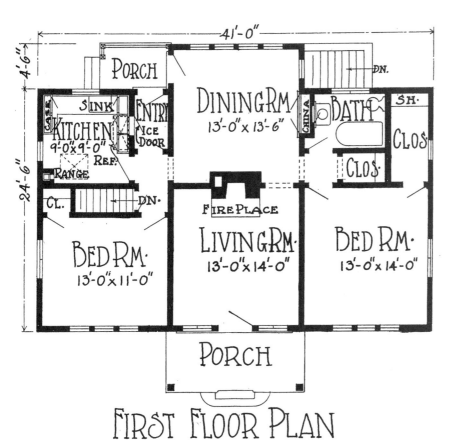

FIRST FLOOR PLAN

EVERY breeze has a full chance at the rooms in this bungalow, for there is a maximum of opening area to the size of the rooms. The windows are both high and low, causing complete clearance of the air in the rooms. There is something inviting about such windows, as you can see from the picture. They give the house a homelike look. Aside from this feature, the plan is unusual and has interesting possibilities. It is especially adapted to the needs of the ultra-modern family in which the woman as well as the man works during the day and a housekeeper is employed perhaps to take care of the house. The family can occupy the bedroom near the bath, while the servant can use the bedroom near the kitchen. Anyone working in one part of the house would not be apt to disturb the occupants of the other part.

The Hollister

SECOND FLOOR

BED RM.
10'-0"x14'-0"

CL.

BATH

CL.

HALL

BED RM.
9'-3"x17'-0"

CL.

CL.

BED RM.
10'-0"x10'-0"

FIRST FLOOR

KITCHEN
9'-6"x10'-0"

PANTRY

SEAT
TABLE
SEAT

CL.

HALL

DINING RM.
13'-6"x16'-0"

LIVING RM.
14'-0"x24'-0"

SUN PORCH

40'-0"

25'-0"

26'-0"

9'-0"

AN UNIQUE SIDE ENTRANCE FOR THE CAR OWNER

The Dumont

PLACING the entrance to The Dumont on the side has done two things: made a very convenient entrance for the family using an automobile and having a driveway from the street; and made it possible to put the smaller dimensions of the house on the street and therefore to build it on a narrower lot. A frontage of 40 feet is plenty for both house and driveway. Note that the entrance itself is on the grade level, but the first floor is four steps up inside the house.

A HAPPY COMBINATION OF BRICK AND STUCCO

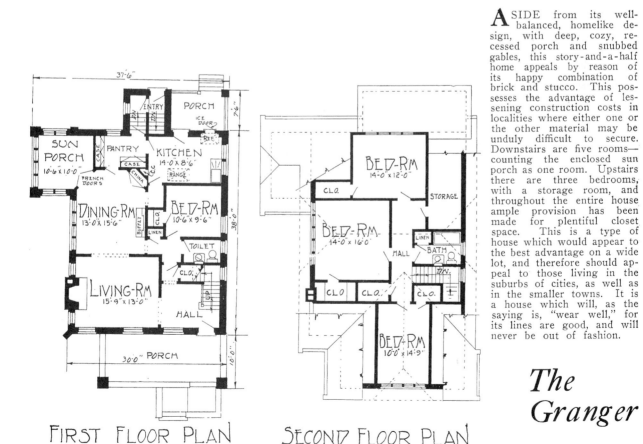

FIRST FLOOR PLAN   SECOND FLOOR PLAN

ASIDE from its well-balanced, homelike design, with deep, cozy, recessed porch and snubbed gables, this story-and-a-half home appeals by reason of its happy combination of brick and stucco. This possesses the advantage of lessening construction costs in localities where either one or the other material may be unduly difficult to secure. Downstairs are five rooms—counting the enclosed sun porch as one room. Upstairs there are three bedrooms, with a storage room, and throughout the entire house ample provision has been made for plentiful closet space. This is a type of house which would appear to the best advantage on a wide lot, and therefore should appeal to those living in the suburbs of cities, as well as in the smaller towns. It is a house which will, as the saying is, "wear well," for its lines are good, and will never be out of fashion.

The Granger

FOR THE LOT WITH AN ATTRACTIVE FRONT VIEW

BECAUSE the living room and dining room occupy the entire front of the house and each has windows on two sides, this is a good house to build where you have a good front view. It is also a good house for a shallow lot, since it is only 31½ feet deep itself. The uncommon ararngement of the front rooms allows an inside hall which completely separates the sleeping quarters from the rest of the house. It also makes a passageway between the kitchen and dining room which will help to keep cooking odors out of the dining room and therefore out of the living room. The pantry is large enough for a breakfast nook if one is preferred. An enclosed stairway leads out of the kitchen to the storage attic above. There is an efficient arrangement of equipment in this kitchen as you can see in the location of the refrigerator and the sink.

The Vincent

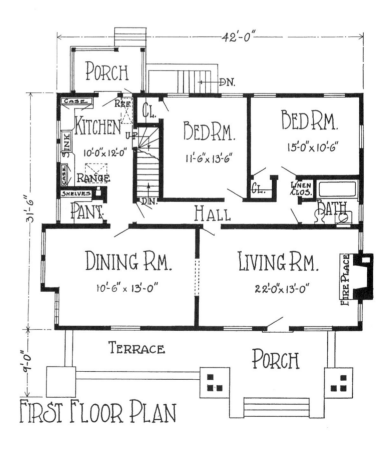

FIRST FLOOR PLAN

THE VERY PLAN FOR THE NARROW CORNER LOT

A CORNER lot has its disadvantages as well as its advantages. Both are recognized in the plan of this house. Except in the dining room, the windows on the side nearest the street are small and high, insuring privacy to the living room. The entrance is on the side rather than through the living porch, leaving the latter undisturbed. With this big living porch, usable the year round, there is no need for a big living room. The side entrance makes possible a convenient reception hall which separates the first floor into two distinct parts. Having the stairway double back on itself produces the same effect upstairs. These second floor bedrooms can be finished later if not needed immediately, for there is a downstairs bedroom with a toilet of its own for the owner's bedroom. In addition to a good sized dining room, The Easton has a breakfast nook just off the kitchen. The daylight pantry is another convenience, since it provides storage space for surplus kitchen supplies.

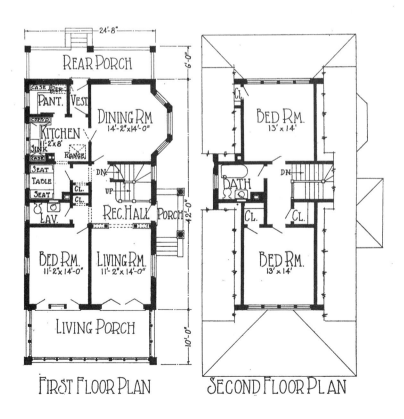

FIRST FLOOR PLAN   SECOND FLOOR PLAN

The Easton

TROY WILL EASILY FIT A FIFTY-FOOT LOT

IN spite of its long, low lines and big rooms, this bungalow is so compact that it can be built on an ordinary 50-foot lot. The arrangement of the bedrooms has many advantages. The second floor rooms can be finished off when they are needed, and when in use there is a special bathroom for them. At the same time, the two main floor chambers will serve a small family and they have their own bathroom, too. The location of the back door or grade entry is where it is convenient to both the kitchen and basement.

The Troy

FIRST FLOOR PLAN

SECOND FLOOR PLAN

FOR THE NARROW CORNER LOT BUT EASILY ADAPTED TO AN INSIDE LOT

BECAUSE of the location of the entrance porch at an angle to the house, this plan is especially fitted to a corner lot, but if the porch is straightened out The Yates will fit a 35-foot inside lot with ease, and if the back porch is omitted will require even less frontage. The plan is a good one for many reasons. You come into a vestibule before entering the living room, an arrangement that keeps cold winds out of the house proper. The fireplace is at one end of the room where it is most usable. Both bedrooms and bath are by themselves, connected with the rest of the house only by a little passage. Each chamber has an exceptionally large closet. You need use the dining room only for formal meals if you like, inasmuch as a large breakfast nook is handy for ordinary meals.

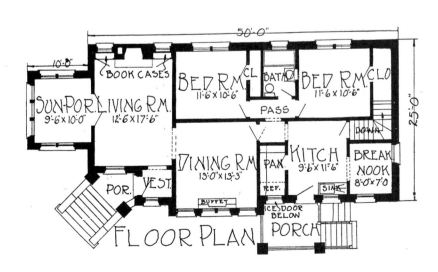

The Yates

49

A RAMBLING PLAN AND DESIGN SUITED TO THE BUNGALOW

ONE of the reasons why the one-story house is popular is because it presents long, low, horizontal lines which suggest repose and quiet, and these are qualities that we associate with the word home. Therefore a plan that is not too hard and fast in outline and that rambles wherever the need for rooms dictates, is apt to shape up into an attractive house. That is the case with The Bixby, where the result is unusually effective, due to the nice proportions of the walls and the restraint shown in the roof, entrance and porch details. In spite of its rambling plan, this bungalow will fit a 50-foot lot.

The Bixby

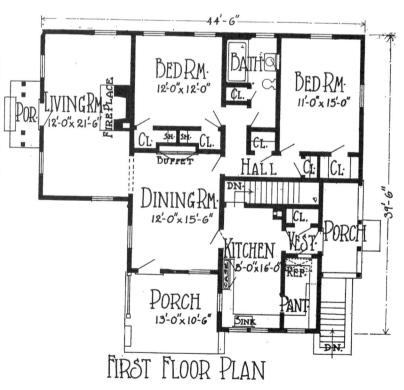

FIRST FLOOR PLAN

A BATHROOM AND BEDROOMS ON EACH FLOOR HERE

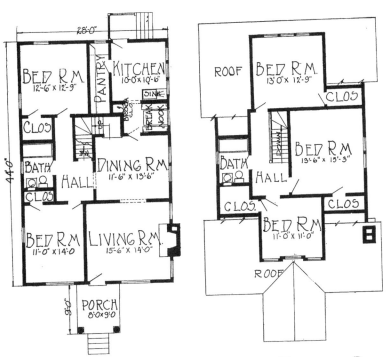

FIRST FLOOR PLAN   SECOND FLOOR PLAN

ALL told there are five bedrooms in The Nashua, two on the first floor and three upstairs. Each floor has a bathroom. Here is comfortable living space; adequate for a large family, or if The Nashua is built as a farm home, for considerable help. The house is a plan that is adaptable to the family that is expected to grow in size. When it is first built perhaps only the downstairs rooms need be finished for occupancy; the bedrooms upstairs can be finished later when needed or as the family's finances permit. There are lots of big closets in this house and one little one whose usefulness will far outstrip its size, and that one is the broom closet near the kitchen. Not only brooms but the carpet sweeper, vacuum cleaner, extra table leaves and lots of things can be kept out of the way here.

The Nashua

A PRIVATE BATHROOM FOR THE MASTER'S BEDROOM

THERE ought never to be any arguments over who is to use the bathroom or when or how long in this house. No one need care how much time the lord and master takes for his shaving, because another bath is always available. That is a convenience that householders are coming more and more to appreciate. Who knows but what the popular house of the future will be one with a bath for every bedroom, just as in the case of the most up-to-date hotels today? Such comforts make for leisurely, decent living and make habits of cleanliness a pleasure instead of a chore. Don't think that the two bathrooms are the only points of value in The Marlow, however. Note also the large living room and the wide pantry between the dining room and kitchen.

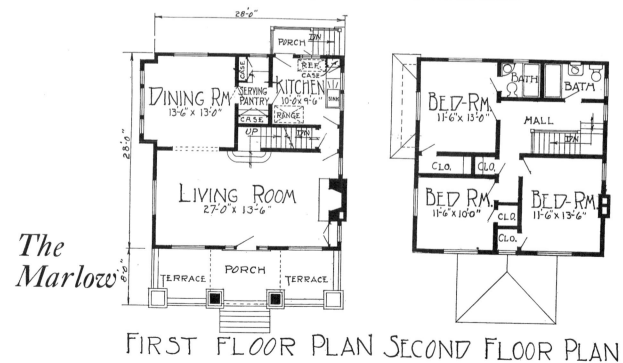

The Marlow

FIRST FLOOR PLAN SECOND FLOOR PLAN

THINK OF IT!   A CIRCULAR STAIRCASE IN A TOWER!

WHY should the stairway be treated in so many houses as a necessary evil? Why shouldn't it be made an architectural feature of the home—of the outside as well as the inside? "Castles in Spain" and other real and imaginary wonder buildings do it. Can't ordinary homes do it, too? The designer of this house thought so, and he went to sure enough Spanish castles for his inspiration for treating the staircase. He put it in a tower, with mysterious little windows lighting the steps, right near the entrance and in front of the house. Thus the stairway is made a thing of beauty and interest when seen from the living room, and there is no space-consuming stair hall on either floor.

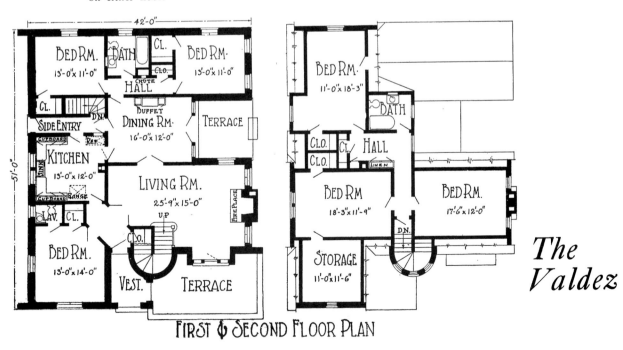

The Valdez

FIRST & SECOND FLOOR PLAN

SECOND FLOOR PLAN

FIRST FLOOR PLAN

BEDROOMS BIG ENOUGH FOR LIVING ROOMS

The Carson

THE CARSON is not a large house, but it has two bedrooms of unusual interest. Each is as large as the living room—itself a large room. Each has space enough for two single beds and two closets. One of these bedrooms is the very thing for the parents with a small child, since the youngster's bedroom immediately adjoins the master's chamber and is directly connected with it. There is a fireplace in this chamber which adds a great deal to its comfort and enjoyment.

54

A FIREPLACE FOR ONE OF THESE BEDROOMS

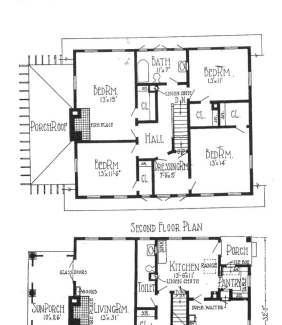

SECOND FLOOR PLAN

FIRST FLOOR PLAN

IT is a great comfort on cold mornings to have a cheerful open fire to dress by. The master's bed-room in The Kenton offers that comfort. Another chamber has a dressing room which can be kept warm over night for dressing in the morning. See what big closets all these bedrooms have; but while you are at it don't neglect the good points of the first floor plan; the spacious living room, the downstairs toilet, the pantry and the big dining room.

The Kenton

FIVE LARGE ROOMS IN A SUITABLE DESIGN FOR A 40-FOOT LOT

UNLESS your needs or fancies are out of the ordinary, you will not care for either a living room or dining room any larger than those in this little bungalow. As to the bedrooms, they are entirely adequate for the usual bedroom furniture, with space enough to spare for reasonable movements in the room. The kitchen is actually larger than some women prefer, but you will find you will probably eat many an informal hurry-up meal there and then you will appreciate its big dimensions. Note this about the bath room: It is 'way back in the back of the house, far removed from the living quarters, yet just across the hall from the bedrooms, where it properly belongs. A clothes chute usable from both bath room and kitchen does away with the cumbersome clothes hamper and heavy lugging of soiled linen on wash days One more point about the fine plan of The Orland: You have access from the outside to the basement and the kitchen through the same door—a convenience on many occasions.

The Orland

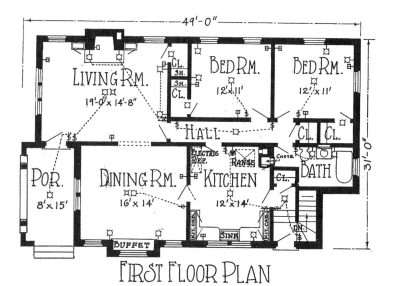

FIRST FLOOR PLAN

OUTDOOR LIVING ROOM IN THIS PORCH ON TWO SIDES OF THE HOUSE

S UCH a porch is bound to be cool most of the time on hot days, if there is a single breath of air stirring. It also keeps the hot sun off the living room walls and so helps to preserve the coolness of that room. This living room has many windows in it, so it can be thrown open to every breeze and made bright as well. To supplement the main heating plant, especially on chilly mornings and evenings in the spring and fall after the furnace is allowed to go out or before it is started, there is a fireplace in the living room. A cased opening connects the living room and dining room and it can be made as wide as you please if you wish to throw these rooms together more.

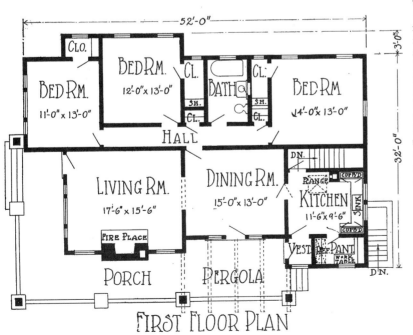

The Kelso

57

EAT ON A BREAKFAST PORCH IN THIS HOUSE

THE ELDRIDGE boasts more than the conventional breakfast nook. It has a porch, enclosed, of course, for breakfast and other informal meals. This porch is directly connected with the living room so it can be used as a living porch, too, when expedient. Good planning is seen in this house in many other details, too, as, for example, the back stairway. It connects with the front stairway at the landing—but is shut off by a door. Every bedroom in The Eldridge has a dressing room.

The Eldridge

FIRST FLOOR PLAN   SECOND FLOOR PLAN

FOR DOCTORS WITH RESIDENCE OFFICES

DOCTORS will look with special favor on this plan, which is especially arranged to fill the needs of the professional man. It gives an 11-foot 3-inch by 9-foot office with an ample sized reception room while the needed toilet and medicine rooms are also well provided for. If followed for residential use, exclusively, the plan permits a downstairs bedroom or a den or library. There are three bedrooms above stairs, all conveniently opening onto the hall and close to the bath. And we dare say that the open porch, with its prepared canvas roofing, might be often used as well as the "front porch." The appearance and roominess of this home will appeal to all.

The Ralston

59

EVERY ROOM BUT THE KITCHEN GETS CROSS-CORNER LIGHT AND VENTILATION

YOU may be able to find some bungalows as small as this and just as well planned, but you won't find many better planned. That is, better planned from the standpoint of light and air for each room, easy communication between them, and economy of construction. Note especially the location of the stairway to the basement. It is equally accessible from the kitchen, living room and bedrooms. No matter where you are in the house it is only a step or two when you must tend the furnace. This situation puts two walls and a hall between the kitchen and living room and so helps to prevent cooking odors and noises reaching the latter. The dining room is not continuous with the living room, but has an existence and importance all its own, and also light and ventilation from windows on three sides. Finally, the bedrooms are by themselves, with the bath conveniently between and separated by a hall from the living quarters.

The Fairfax

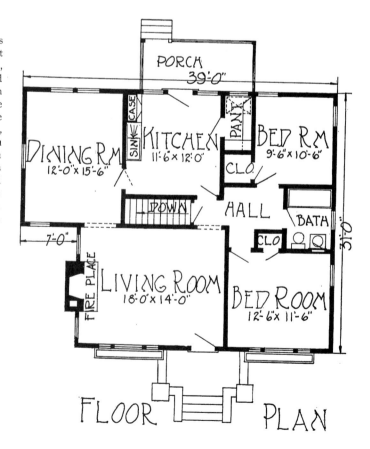

EXTRA ROOMS OR STORAGE ATTIC UPSTAIRS, WHICHEVER YOU MOST NEED

ONLY the first floor plan is shown here but another room or two can be arranged on the second floor if you want it, or you can use the space as storage room if you prefer. The stairway goes up out of the reception hall, but it is completely enclosed and shut off by a door and you would never suspect that there was a stairway. To save space and cost the basement stairway goes down underneath this one, and in this situation is very handy to the kitchen. You will notice that there is an outside basement stairway, too, under cover of the back porch. It is for use when carrying out ashes or on wash days, taking a lot of traffic out of the kitchen. Although each bedroom has a closet, there is additional closet space in the hall. Putting the living and dining rooms both in the front of the house, insures the best outlook for these important rooms when built on the ordinary city lot.

The Indianola

61

EASY TO BUILD, LIVE IN, PAY FOR, RENT OR SELL

ALL because it is so small as to dimensions, yet big as to rooms. You can get this house on a 30-foot lot, yet it has a living room that would suggest a house twice as large. All the other rooms are entirely adequate for ordinary family use. It is careful planning which has enabled them to be so large in such a small house. No space is wasted in halls, and the walls and roof of the house are of straight construction, making construction easy and inexpensive. Yet, because of the attractiveness of the design and the liveableness of the plan The Deerfield is a bungalow that would appeal immediately to the renter or buyer looking for a distinctive small house. Therefore if you build it to live in you will find your profits in your enjoyment of it, and if you build it to rent or sell, in the return on your investment.

The
Deerfield

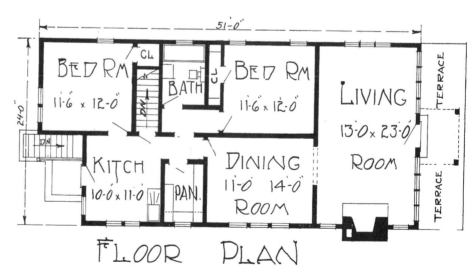

FLOOR PLAN

ANOTHER WELL PLANNED SMALL HOUSE TO BUILD TO RENT OR SELL

THE KEOTA will need a lot a little wider than 30 feet in most localities, but not much. And with the gable ends parallel with the street the house looks larger than it really is, although no one can object to the size of the rooms inside, because they do not belie the promise of the exterior. The living room extends clear across the front and has windows on three sides which give it abundance of light and air and allow full views of the street. The dining room is larger than usual in houses 25 feet wide and so are the bedrooms. The generous dimensions of these rooms are due partly to the absence of useless wall space. A mere passage connects the bedrooms and bath here and these rooms with the rest of the house. It is a good arrangement to have the kitchen and dining room separated a little as here, since then it is difficult for cooking odors to announce your menu to waiting guests.

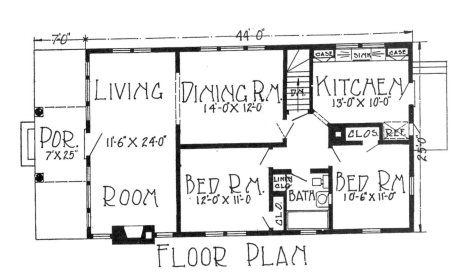

FLOOR PLAN

The Keota

A COLONIAL BUNGALOW OF UNIQUE DESIGN

THIS is a thoroughly well-handled small bungalow, and while it draws on our Colonial period for its general design it possesses an individuality of its own. The gayly colored awnings help, of course; they make an excellent contrast to the white painted wide Colonial siding. Then, too, the gracefully arched near-dormers in the roof help a great deal, and afford ventilation to the attic likewise. The porch has bricked steps and the front door opens directly into the living room, with its fireplace and built-in bookcases. Off it is the dining room, with built-in-buffet, and off this are the kitchen and the pantry. The latter has a window, ample shelving and an outside icing door. There are two bedrooms, with bathroom adjoining, and a rear porch. Worth noting is how shrubbery improves this bungalow and lot.

The Lindsay

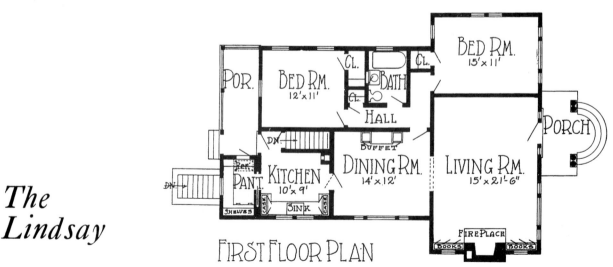

FIRST FLOOR PLAN

FLOOR PLAN

MORE BEDROOMS UPSTAIRS IF YOU NEED THEM

ALTHOUGH there are three bedrooms and a bathroom on the first floor of this house, there is space for two more rooms and a toilet or bathroom on the second floor, if you need the room. The Walker is a bit out of the ordinary in the matter of its entrance. The entrance steps are inside the house where they are protected from rain and snow and ice, instead of outside.

The Walker

EVERY SQUARE INCH OF SPACE IN THIS HOUSE IS MADE USEFUL

JUST look at this plan and see what it offers you in addition to eight major rooms. On the first floor you get a big front porch, a toilet for the maid's room, a reception hall with a coat closet, a closet and fireplace for the living room, and in the kitchen a pantry, vestibule and rear porch. Upstairs you have broad balconies, both front and rear, directly accessible from the bedrooms, private toilets for the two rear bedrooms and the master's room, with an extraordinarily large bathroom to serve the house. The tub in this room is recessed, suggesting the built-in type of tub and possibly shower equipment. Did you ever before see so many conveniences and comforts in a house whose main body is less than 25 feet wide?

The Monticello

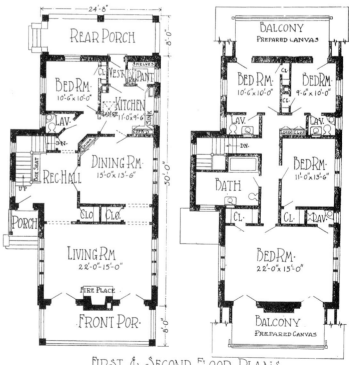

FIRST & SECOND FLOOR PLANS

66

PRIVATE LAVATORIES FOR TWO OF THESE BEDROOMS AND ANOTHER ONE DOWNSTAIRS

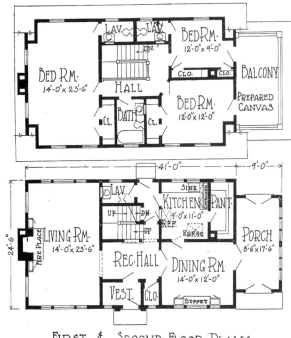

FIRST & SECOND FLOOR PLANS

BEFORE you look at the first floor plan of The Hinckley, see what a carefully planned second floor it has. The master's bedroom is luxuriously large and strictly up-to-date in that it has a private toilet at one end and a wardrobe closet at the other. Wardrobes are insisted upon by many discriminating home owners, because they are more usable than most closets. The small bedroom also has a private toilet and is therefore ideal as a guest room. The closet in this room might have two doors on the long side and open up as a wardrobe, too, as in the master's bedroom, if you prefer. The third bedroom has a wardrobe closet also. On the first floor The Hinckley is just as carefully thought out. You see this in the hall closet, the kitchen pantry and the placing of the stairway running parallel with the length of the house.

The Hinckley

A SIMPLE, CONSERVATIVE DESIGN IN THE SPANISH STYLE

NOTE how frankly this roof is treated. It is just a roof—a tile roof. It does not overpower the structure beneath. That is why you like it. You will like it more and more the more you see of it. The walls are well proportioned; no foundation line is visible and the stucco extends clear to the ground. Arched openings in the front facade, a rough trowel finish for the stucco and a little wrought iron work, are the details which, with the tile roof, give this bungalow a decided Spanish touch. The tall casements are characteristic of the style. On the inside they make cool rooms in the summer. The porch is not the least of the desirable features of The Rochelle.

The Rochelle

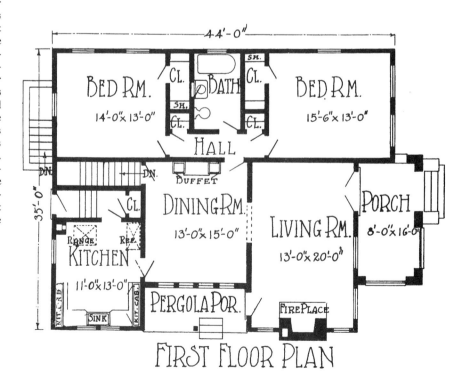

FIRST FLOOR PLAN

LIVING ROOM AND DINING ROOM CAN BE THROWN TOGETHER

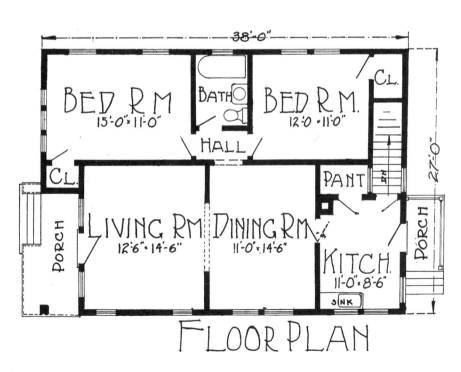

FLOOR PLAN

BECAUSE a wide cased opening joins the living room and dining room, these two rooms can be used as one when you are giving a party and want plenty of space for chairs or tables or both. Ordinarily, though, the living room is large enough for the requirements of the small family, and the dining room can be used as a living room by the rest of the family when one member is entertaining callers in the living room. Then, too, a bed and other ordinary bedroom furniture will go in the master's bedroom with space enough to spare for a chair or two and perhaps a small table. Thus you can see the possibilities of this good plan.

*The
Vernon*

POSSIBILITIES OF THE L-SHAPED LIVING ROOM

HAVE you thought such an unusual thing as that kind of living room an impossibility for the small house? This room in The Geneva is of interesting layout. There is a big bay by the fireplace that will allow the family circle to gather around in comfort. Perhaps at the far end of the room you can put your piano; or you can have books there and a table, as in a library. There is plenty of wall space for an effective arrangement of furniture.

*The
Geneva*

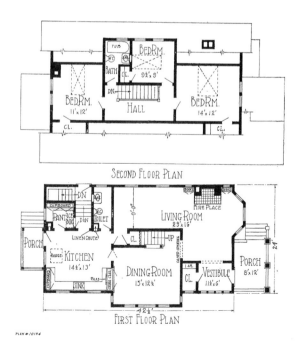

SECOND FLOOR PLAN

FIRST FLOOR PLAN

PLAN # 10154

FACE THIS HOUSE ANY WAY YOU PLEASE

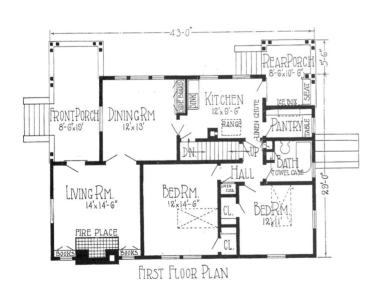

FIRST FLOOR PLAN

THE only room that might suffer if the house faced north is the dining room, since the porch would reduce the light received from the front window. But the room has another window—three of them—which will be sufficient for light in all seasons. With the exception of one chamber every room has the advantage of cross-corner ventilation and light. You go down to the basement directly from the kitchen and the attic stair is accessible from the bedroom hall.

The Tecumseh

71

DO YOU NEED A DEN, OFFICE OR SPARE ROOM?

IF you do, The Urbana has it for you. You enter the room directly from the vestibule and it can be shut off from the living room by a sliding door so that if used as an office it has absolute privacy. On the other hand there is a closet in the room in which a fold-up bed on rollers can be kept so that an emergency bedroom can be made of it when necessary. Such a spare room is always a desirable adjunct to any house but you would hardly expect to find it in this small house. It is not, however, the most important thing about The Urbana. The exterior design is the outstanding quality of this house. The roof of variegated colored shingles, the arched entrance, the blinds and the window cages are details that make a most attractive facade. Build the house low on the ground and in the same proportion you see here and you will get the same results.

The Urbana

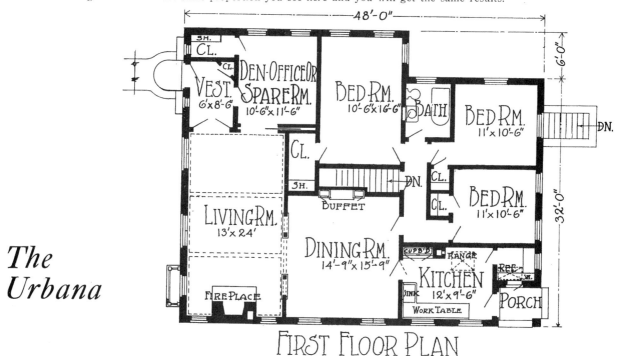

FIRST FLOOR PLAN

PLENTY OF LIGHT AND VENTILATION FOR THESE FRONT ROOMS

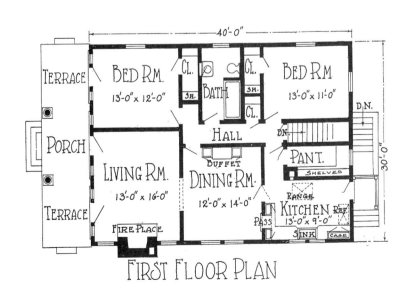

FIRST FLOOR PLAN

INSTEAD of ordinary windows in the front of The Trowbridge, French doors with sidelights to correspond are used and they make bright rooms inside and afford abundant ventilation on hot days. The effect, with the open terrace which runs clear across the front of the house, is interesting. It is possible to get a clean sweep of breezes clear through the living portion of this house by opening up the dining room and kitchen doors. Each of the bedrooms, on the other hand, has cross-corner ventilation. Notice the big closets in these chambers. You can make wardrobes out of these closets by putting another door in each and hanging your clothes on a rod running lengthwise of the closets.

The
Trowbridge

MODIFIED DUTCH COLONIAL

THE pleasing and practical features of the Dutch Colonial type of home, so long associated with brick and frame construction, have been utilized in a stucco dwelling, which is presented here. The first floor is planned in the conventional Colonial manner, with the hall containing the stairs dividing the long, spacious living room from the dining room and kitchen. On the second floor are two pleasant bedrooms, lighted from two sides, and a hall bath, with the master's room and its private bath across the hall.

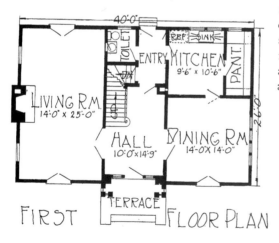

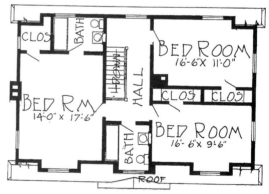

The Montague

A   STUCCO   AND   FRAME   HOME

THIS home, with the first story of stucco and the second of frame construction, contains many of the features of Colonial architecture, particularly in the arrangement of the rooms. The combination of the porch with a terrace on both sides and the French doors opening on the terrace are interesting details of this exterior. The central hall has the living room on one side and the dining room and kitchen on the other. A maid's room and bath are provided on the first floor. On the second floor are three adequate bedrooms and two baths.

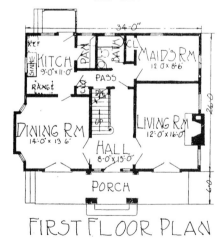

FIRST FLOOR PLAN

SECOND FLOOR PLAN

The Dwight

INDOORS AND OUT THIS IS A HOME

W HAT could be more popular than this well shaded,
yet open, side porch? It is away from the public's
gaze and looks out on a landscape that is well kept and
therefore beautiful. The entrance, too, is attractive because of its substantial simplicity. No eye could miss
or fail to admire the dormer windows. The living room,
dining room and pergola porch open into each other,
while the bedrooms are so placed as to avoid the noises
of the streets. The accessibility of the icebox and pantry
is another commendable feature.

The Cimarron

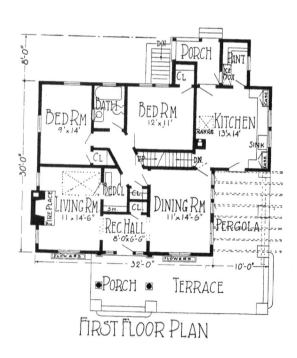

FIRST FLOOR PLAN

WOULD YOU LIKE A BIG LINEN CLOSET IN THE BATHROOM

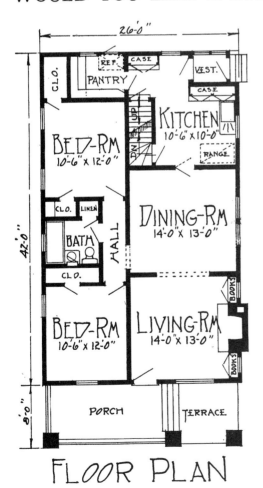

FLOOR PLAN

THAT is really the place for linen, especially towels and wash cloths, as well as soap and other bathroom supplies. Quite a large linen closet is provided in the bathroom of The Farmington, and there are good closets for the bedrooms, too. A useful contrivance for a deep closet like that in the back bedroom is a device which allows the clothes to be hung on hangers from a rod, and the whole rod, clothes and all, can be pulled out into the room, so you don't have to go into the closet to get the garment you want. The closet in the front bedroom might have two doors instead of one, closing toward each other. Thus would the whole expanse of the closet be thrown open for your inspection when getting out your clothes.

The Farmington

FRONT AND BACK STAIRWAY IN ONE

SPACE has been saved and useless steps avoided by the stair arrangement in this house. The main stair is accessible from the kitchen as well as the front hall, and since it is only three steps up to the landing, the effect is practically the same as a hall. That means direct access from the kitchen to the front door is possible without going around through the pantry, dining room and living room.

The Newcomb

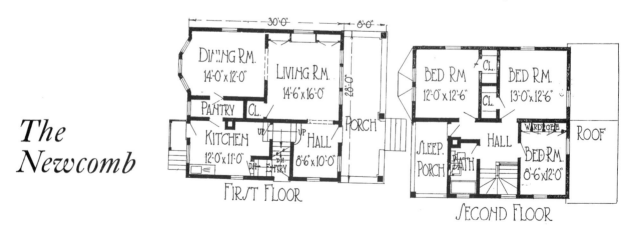

AN ATTRACTIVE ENGLISH-STYLE RESIDENCE

YOU have perhaps noticed that a peculiarity of houses designed after the English cottage type is that there is no provision for porches. In this case awnings supply that deficiency somewhat, and a terrace with pergola which you see at the right. There are, of course, advantages pro and con, with respect to the porch, but in hot and continuously warm climates a cool interior is often to be preferred to an outer porch with its warmer outer air. In this house our arched front recessed entrance porch leads into a hall, with the dining room on the left and the living room on the right, and the kitchen directly ahead at the end of the hall passage. Observe that the sleeping chambers are at the rear of the house, and except for a door opening through from the kitchen, are shut off completely from the day-rooms proper. This house, which is 37 feet by 38 feet, will appear at best advantage in the midst of trees and shrubbery on a fair sized lot.

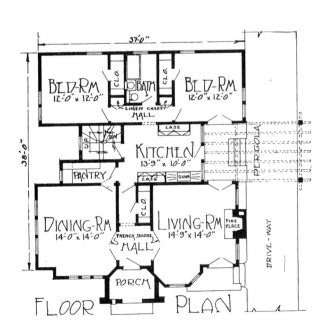

FLOOR PLAN

The Henderson

79

LOTS OF HOUSE FOR THE MONEY IN THIS PRACTICAL PLAN

YOU would hardly guess from outside appearances that this is a six-room house, yet it is, and the rooms are livable in size, too, in spite of the fact that the house itself is only 833 square feet on the ground. It is careful planning that gives you so much house for the money as you get here. You will find yourself more and more appreciative of the design of The Dayton, too, because it is a really good design. The break in the roof that forms the gambrel is well done and the negligible extension of the roof over the gable ends is in keeping with the real old Dutch Colonial architecture.

The Dayton

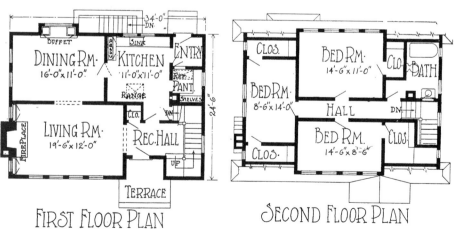

MAID'S ROOM AND LAVATORY ON THE FIRST FLOOR

THE Kingsley is not only planned for the comfort and convenience of the family but also for the help. The maid's room—a corner bedroom with windows on two sides—is next to the kitchen but is not directly connected with the kitchen, which is proper. The downstairs lavatory, while for general use, being conveniently at the end of the hall, is handy to this chamber. The main bedrooms upstairs have easy access to the commodious bathroom. Two hall closets for linens, brooms and household minutiae are conveniences of the upstairs hall. The Kingsley has a large living room with fireplace and a glazed-in sunporch opens from it and from the dining room.

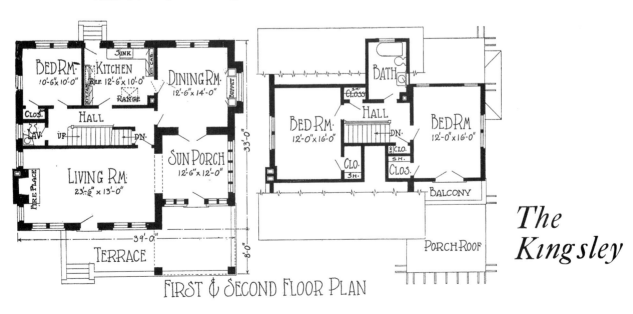

The Kingsley

FIRST & SECOND FLOOR PLAN

A   BRICK   DUTCH   COLONIAL

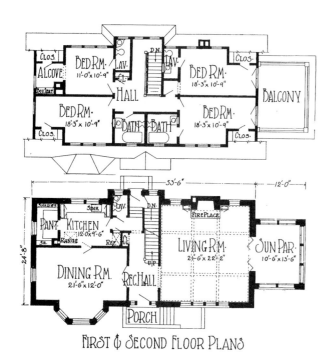

FIRST & SECOND FLOOR PLANS

A PLAN offering many advantages for the larger families is presented here. The designers of this home, while retaining the distinctive features of the Dutch Colonial have modified it to suit their requirements, as is shown in the entryway, so planned that the house may be built along the length of the lot, with the sunporch facing the street. The seven rooms are exceptionally well arranged for comfort and convenience.

The Parnell

HAVE WARDROBES IN THESE BEDROOMS IF YOU LIKE

EACH of the closets of the two bedrooms in The Scotia is so shaped that it can be converted into a wardrobe. Sufficient wall space is left in the rooms for ordinary bedroom furniture even if these chambers do have cross-corner light and ventilation. All the rooms in this bungalow are big, even the kitchen, where there is space enough for a table and chairs for breakfasts and informal meals.

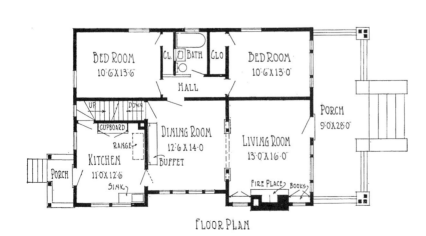

FLOOR PLAN

The Scotia

83

CHARMING, COMPACT FIVE-ROOM BUNGALOW

THERE is something unusually pleasing and distinctive about this delightful little home with its stucco and frame exterior. The long narrow casement windows in living room and dining room afford plenty of light and air to these rooms as well as lend additional charm to the general appearance. The front porch is recessed under a continuation of the main roof and can be screened in during the warm months. The bungalow is 30 feet wide and 38 feet long.

The Lancaster

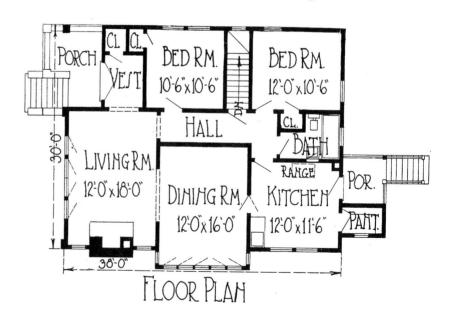

FLOOR PLAN

DARING USE OF THE ARCH IN A SIMPLE DESIGN

S O plain are the walls of this house that those big arches seem just the thing to make the design interesting. There is no need for anything else. The window blinds and the lap siding in the peak of the gable over the living room windows are delightful touches, too. You will like this house the more you see of it; like a good piece of music or a good book, it will wear well. It will be in as good taste a generation from now as it is today, and you, the builder, will never be censured for your old-fashioned taste as many of the older generation living yet are censured today by their heirs. The plan of The Cromwell is as good as its design and is particularly convenient, with the entrance, vestibule and porch where they are, for the car owner who must reach his garage from the street. The house, drive and all, in spite of their appearance to the contrary, will go on a 40-foot lot.

FLOOR PLAN — DRIVE WAY

The Cromwell

NO NEED FOR A SUN PARLOR IN THE LAUREL

THAT is because of the wide bay window of the living room. Practically the entire front end of this roof is a sun parlor as it is. Then, too, The Laurel offers you a long deep, front porch. There is a toilet for the downstairs bedroom which is accessible from the hall, and a big pantry with refrigerator for outside icing intervening between the kitchen and dining room.

The Laurel

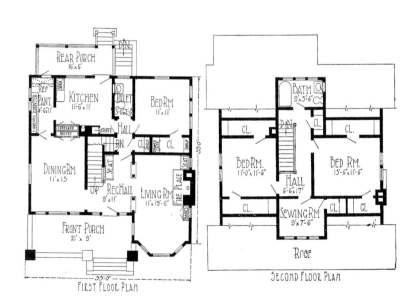

COZY, HOSPITABLE, FIVE-ROOM BUNGALOW

A MOST charming little home with its delightful inviting entrance and well-designed exterior. It embodies an excellent combination of charm, substantial construction and efficient floor plan arrangement, and should prove irresistible in its appeal to home-lovers of all types. The artistic front entrance, set under a gabled hood at the rear of the well-balanced terrace, beckons the passersby.

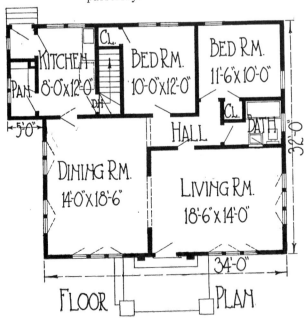

The Harwood

INDIVIDUAL TREATMENT FOR SQUARE HOUSE

The Orleans

EVERYONE knows the advantages of the square house but their very commonness may deter some from building. This design is shown as an example of how individuality can be put into the square house at no extra cost and perhaps at a saving. There is nothing here to cost extra unless it is the stones around the entrance and the rather elaborate front door itself. The principal features of this design are of French origin, but the real beauty lies in the good proportions of the house itself and the fine balance shown in the spacing and treatment of the openings.

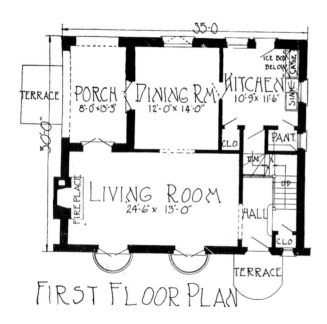

FIRST FLOOR PLAN

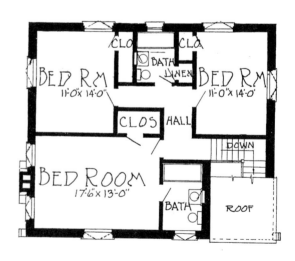

SECOND FLOOR PLAN

A CAREFULLY PLANNED BUNGALOW FOR THE NARROW LOT

THOSE who are seeking the comfort and convenience which has done so much to make the bungalow a type of home built in all parts of America will find them in this plan at a moderate cost. The exterior is a combination of shingles and clapboard, so much favored in a number of communities. The wide porch and the bay in the dining room are features which prevent monotony in the lines of the home. The living room, which is entered directly from the porch, has cross lighting and ventilation and at the same time presents unbroken wall surfaces which will allow attractive grouping of furniture. The dining room is directly behind the living room and is of generous proportions and well lighted. In the kitchen of this home, a great deal of care has been expended in arranging properly the equipment. The bedroom group is well planned. The hall to the rooms takes no space from the rooms themselves and is provided with two closets. The bathroom is insulated from both bedrooms by closets.

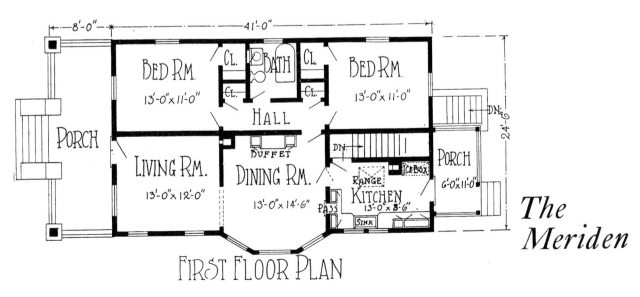

FIRST FLOOR PLAN

The Meriden

TWO FRONTS FOR THIS STORY-AND-A-HALF HOUSE

IT makes little difference whether you put the living room-dining room side of this house to the street or the side with the living room and bedroom. The house will look well in either case and the porch and entrance will be just as usable. The Felton, you notice, is more nearly square than many story-and-a-half houses, which not only means that it has lots of room inside for the lineal feet of wall that you must build, but that the house will fit almost any kind of a lot, that is a shallow lot, a deep one, a lot that slopes from the street to the back or vice versa, or just a plain, level ordinary lot. In other words, it is a pretty adaptable plan and the man who builds to sell or rent and constructs houses in quantities will be apt to be interested in it as well as the man who builds the house for his own home. Look at the plan inside: There is an absence of hall space, the living room having absorbed part of it and the rest going into a small but adequate downstairs bedroom; there is a toilet on the first floor and a pantry in addition to the three regulation rooms; and upstairs a sleeping porch supplements the space of the smaller bedroom.

The Felton

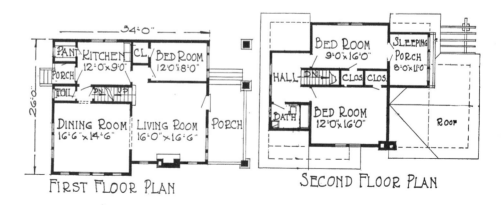

"A GEM FOR ANY SETTING"

A SNAPPY-LOOKING stucco home of economical lines with sun parlor. The room arrangement of this dwelling has been carefully planned and as a result the house seems quite large, although the actual dimensions are only 28 by 37 feet. On the first floor there are four rooms and sun parlor, not to mention a fair-sized front porch. The fourth room can be used either as a den or bedroom as the owner sees fit. Folding or accordion doors separate the dining room from the sun porch which can be used as a breakfast room. Three bedrooms are located on the second floor and all three open out on to balconies.

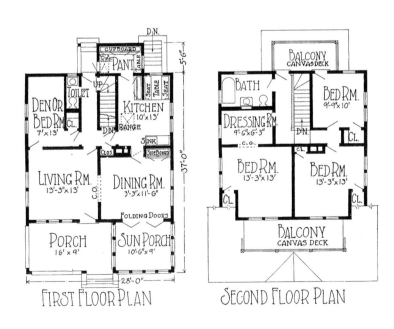

FIRST FLOOR PLAN   SECOND FLOOR PLAN

The Webster

A DESIGN BORROWED FROM A SUNNY CLIMATE ADAPTABLE ANYWHERE

THIS is the kind of house you see in California and Florida and frequently throughout the south. The design is derived from the old Spanish Mission style of architecture. It has decided virtues in its simplicity and the striking color effects which it permits. And with modern materials the flat roof can be made to withstand the heavy snows of colder climates. Such roofs are used without question on apartment houses, factories, schools and other buildings, so why not on individual homes? The severity of the front facade of The Nevada is relieved by the use of roof tile over the entrance to the porch and the mullioned window of the living room. This tile, with its deep color, contrasts vividly with the even tone of the walls. The Nevada has a plan of considerable interest. This is evident especially in the sleeping quarters. These rooms are entirely secluded and the bathroom, while placed where it is not visible from either the dining room or living room, is really as handy to the rest of the house as it is the bedroom.

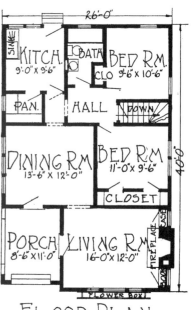

FLOOR PLAN

The Nevada

USE THE DINING ROOM AND LIVING ROOM AS ONE BIG ONE ON SPECIAL OCCASIONS

AS you can see from both the picture and floor plan, The Jasper is not a large house, but closer inspection will show you that when the occasion demands you have available some 434 square feet of floor space as a living room. That is enough for rather large parties; many a private ballroom floor is no larger. This is possible because instead of a door or several doors only a wide cased opening connects the dining room and living room. This opening can be hung with curtains, so that the two rooms can be shut off from each other completely at other times. Another example of thoughtful placing of the openings in this house is in the connection between the dining room and kitchen. You pass through the pantry instead of directly. That makes is impossible for the diner to see into the kitchen when anyone is passing in or out of the kitchen and it keeps the aromas of cooking from penetrating the house.

FLOOR PLAN

The Jasper

LOOK WHAT A BREAKFAST PORCH IS HERE!

I T is nearly as large as the dining room and is directly connected with the kitchen. French doors open upon it from the living room, so it can be used as a sun parlor or living porch if you like. Another interesting detail of the first floor of The Barnard is the stairway. Although a closed stair, the three lower steps are open on both sides, making an architectural feature of importance to both the living room and dining room.

The Barnard

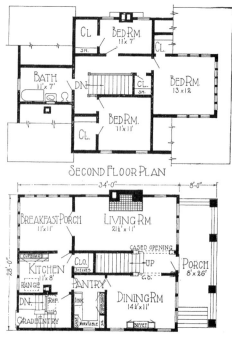

SECOND FLOOR PLAN

FIRST FLOOR PLAN

FIRST FLOOR PLAN.

SECOND FLOOR PLAN

EIGHT MAJOR ROOMS BUT ONLY 26½ FEET WIDE!

EXAMINE this plan, both floors of it, carefully for there is more room here than
you will expect. And the fine part of it is that the living room and master's bedroom have not been cut down in size to make space for less important rooms. Most
families like to have these two rooms big and their wishes have been taken into consid-
eration in this plan. The house is 26½ by 46½ without the front porch.

The
Prescott

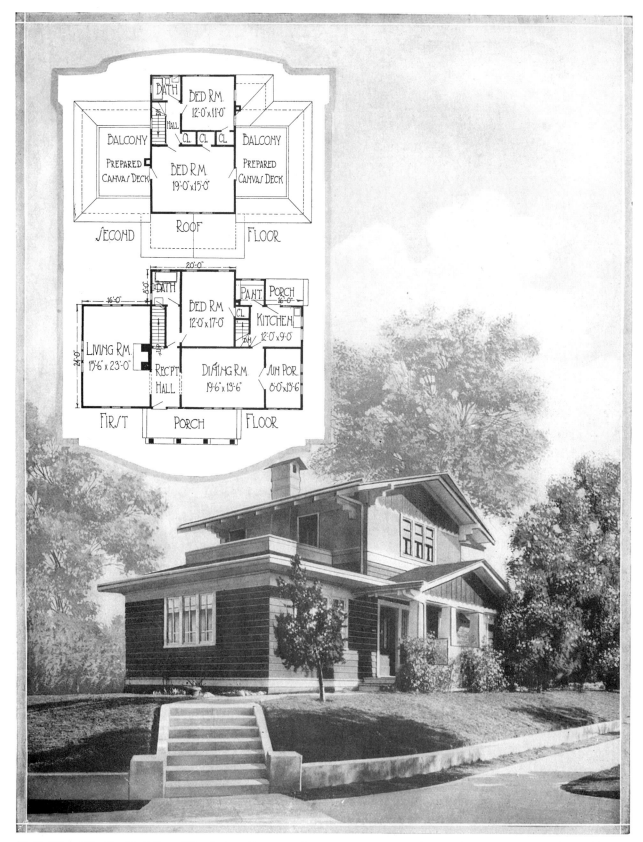

In the floor plans:

SECOND FLOOR

- BATH
- BED RM. 12'-0" x 11'-0"
- HALL
- BALCONY — PREPARED CANVAS DECK
- CL. CL. CL.
- BED RM. 19'-0" x 15'-0"
- BALCONY — PREPARED CANVAS DECK
- ROOF

SECOND ··· ROOF ··· FLOOR

FIRST FLOOR

- BATH
- 20'-0"
- 6'-0"
- BED RM. 12'-0" x 17'-0"
- PANT.
- PORCH 16'-0"
- CL.
- KITCHEN 12'-0" x 9'-0"
- 16'-0"
- 24'-0"
- LIVING RM. 15'-6" x 23'-0"
- RECP'T HALL
- DINING RM. 19'-6" x 13'-6"
- SUN POR. 8'-0" x 13'-6"

FIRST ··· PORCH ··· FLOOR

SIX-ROOM HOUSE OF UNUSUAL DESIGN

The Abingdon

HERE is a home that will appeal very strongly to those who are seeking something different. Built along the so-called "airplane" lines which are so popular in the West, it has many features that tend to make it unique. The cupola effect of the second floor is one of these. At either end is a balcony covered with prepared canvas, **a very** popular flooring and roofing material. Two bedrooms are located on the second floor. On the lower floor are the living room, ample and comfortable dining room, bedroom and kitchen, also a sun parlor.